YOUR PATH TO
Inspiration

KIRA HARLAMOR

Copyright © 2024 Kira Harlamor.

Photography by Kira Harlamor.

All rights reserved. No part of this book may be reproduced, stored, or transmitted by any means—whether auditory, graphic, mechanical, or electronic—without written permission of both publisher and author, except in the case of brief excerpts used in critical articles and reviews. Unauthorized reproduction of any part of this work is illegal and is punishable by law.

ISBN: 979-8-89419-373-1 (sc)
ISBN: 979-8-89419-374-8 (hc)
ISBN: 979-8-89419-375-5 (e)

Because of the dynamic nature of the Internet, any web addresses or links contained in this book may have changed since publication and may no longer be valid. The views expressed in this work are solely those of the author and do not necessarily reflect the views of the publisher, and the publisher hereby disclaims any responsibility for them.

One Galleria Blvd., Suite 1900, Metairie, LA 70001
(504) 702-6708

I'm very thankful for my family and friends that have been there for support throughout my life. I love to be inspired and to inspire others. I'm dedicating this particular photo book to my fabulous friend, David Perea_Artist in SF, who not only showed support but also encouragement which allowed me to conquer and fulfill one of my life goals. I used the Author Name of, "Loves2sing11" for this book as well. I decided to use my on-line dating name which is another fabulous story of how I met David, so it all ties into one another in many ways. I love to sing and my favorite number is lucky 11. Once again, I thank you for entering my life, allowing my passions to flow and helping me share them with others...You are an inspiration!!!

Always choose the best path for you!!!

Learn not to quickly judge!!!

Allow time to play it's role!!!

Allow yourself personal growth each year!!!

*Building bridges is a skill,
so is crossing them!!!*

Beautiful taste, smell, sight of red and white!!!

Always have continuous flow!!!

Amazing path towards a beautiful life!!!

Inspiration comes in many forms!!!

Continue to rise to your top!!!

We must cross bridges to our destinations!!!

Sit back, relax and let the light shine on!!!

Looking up imagining!!!

Staying calm is a learned virtue...pass it on!!!

Enchanting, exquisite complexion... purple hues!!!

*Grass can always be greener
if you want it to!!!*

Relax to this sensational sunset! Breathe deep!!!

Delightful radiance of peace and serenity!!!

Happiness...that everlasting spiritual moment!!!

Embrace your purpose in life and manifest!!!

Life is an increase in elevation...
so don't fall...rise!!!

Keep peace within yourself during chaos!!!

Defog your mind and feel the gentle breeze!!!

When mountains block your path, spread your wings and fly over them!!!

Allow your life to be that beautiful song and sing!!!

Create your happiness on purpose!!!

When it's 1111 make a wish!!!

Sing and let your passions flow with Kira Harlamor!!!

Loves2sing11

www.ingramcontent.com/pod-product-compliance
Lightning Source LLC
LaVergne TN
LVHW070442070526
838199LV00036B/681